Seduce Me!

What Women Really Want

R. Gregory Alonzo

D1057719

A Chambers Book
California
2nd Edition
Revised

Copyright 2003 by R. Gregory Alonzo
Published by Chambers Books

Cover Model: Juli Becker

Photos By Zarek

Cover design by Creative Solutions

Image Consultant: Heather Cooper-Smith

Library of Congress
Catalog in Publication Data
Alonzo, R. Gregory
Seduce Me! What Women Really Want

ISBN 0-9744916-9-1

Printed in the United States of America

"Some day I hope to write a book where the royalties will pay for the copies I give away."

Clarence Darrow

Acknowledgments

Arabian horses and the vine covered slopes of the Santa Ynez Valley. This is my place. It is where I go for rest, reflection and rejuvenation. It is the most appropriate place to acknowledge the many who made this book possible. Cassidy Boyd, Bruce Fredenburg, John Lotspeich, Bonnie Prusa, Rick Rojo, John Sherer and Louise Tenbrook Whiting. They are not only my colleagues, they are my friends. They provided the inspiration to make this book a reality.

R. Gregory Alonzo
August 2003
Santa Ynez, CA

For Her

Contents

Foreword

If you are looking for ideas to increase your dating I.Q. and want to get tips that really work, this book is for you. Get ready to give up all of the old ideas about women and men that haven't worked for you and get ready to have more fun.

When I was a college freshman, I found a book on how to seduce women, written by a psychologist. Much to my surprise, it was a far deeper and more useful book than the title implied. This book by R. Gregory Alonzo, "Seduce Me! What Women Really Want", is in the same vein. It actually contains useful information on understanding the dating ritual in realistic terms. Greg teaches the reader how to improve their dating and love life with straight-up tips that really work, without asking the reader to do anything ridiculous or demeaning. I have known Greg for more than 10 years, and I can assure you he has tested out every idea in this book, and they all work.

Bruce R. Fredenburg, M.S., L.M.F.T.

Author of *Women Good: Men Bad?*

Prologue

"I always meet women because of one simple truth...
I know that success is mine before I set out."*

R. Gregory Alonzo

A glimmer of light fell over her and illuminated those emerald eyes. The sight of her took my breath away. Pausing to collect myself, I knew that she was the one, the woman of my most favorite desires. I watched with longing as she chuckled softly, her hair falling forward in golden swathes.

Throwing my shoulders back, I drew myself to full height and strode briskly to her. "Excuse me," I smiled with self assurance " When I saw you," my eyes crinkled into a smile. " I said to myself, now there's a woman I'd like to meet... My name is Greg," extending my hand in friendship, "Greg Alonzo."

Momentarily taken aback, she accepted my outstretched palm. Smiling demurely, she said, " My name is Karla."

Part One

What Do Women Want?

Chapter One

What Do Women Want?

"Chance makes a play thing of a man's life"
Seneca

*"A man's reach should exceed his grasp,
or what's a heaven for"*
Robert Browning

The simple truth is that most men just don't realize that meeting, seducing and bedding women can be surprisingly simple. Women love sex as much as men. It pains me to watch those of you who foul up easy opportunities to get the fairer sex into bed.

This is why I interviewed hundreds of women, experts and sexperts to arm my readers with everything needed to know about meeting and seducing women. I would also point out that each woman's name has been changed for privacy and to protect the name of guilty.

Colleen, 29, Image Consultant, Hollywood, California

"I loved the story you told in the prologue about how you approached Karla. Men usually come up to us spouting some horrific line. If you expect to get anywhere with me, idle chitchat is a big...big mistake."

Seduce Me!

Helen, 31, Commercial Realtor, Baltimore, Maryland

"It's because they have no conception as to what we women want. I find it so refreshing when a man simply comes up and introduces himself."

What then do women want? This is where we must begin if we are ever to find success on the dating scene.

Over the years much has been written on the subject of the difference between men and women. Though true, don't let this fact intimidate you. With continued use of this simple guide, you will meet more women and score much more often.

In order to be successful with women, there are three questions that we men must know the answers:

1. What do women find irresistible in men?

2. What turns women off?

3. How to push a women's lust buttons?

Experts agree that all women are looking for some basic qualities in men. Women do have their types, however, the same handful of characteristics lie at the heart of all women's wish lists.

Kara, 32, Media Consultant, New York City

"I want a man with a proven track record. With that, I'm looking for viable resources. This is not to say that I am only interested in a man's fiscal health, success is alluring. When a man is successful, it shows that he goes after and gets what he wants. I absolutely love being seduced by a confident man."

Throughout my conversations with women like Kara, who are attracted to a man's "resources," education also proved to be a romantic turn on.

Debra, 28, Realtor, Tucson, Arizona

"Successful men tend to be better-educated and witty. They have a sense of themselves and are more attentive in bed."

Paula, 30, Loan Consultant, Newport Beach, California

"I used to date this Stanford Magna. He had it all. The BMW, Italian suits and a condo at the beach. Yet what really made me fall for him was that he was a great conversationalist. He seemed to always know what to say and never talked down at me. I learned a lot from him. Not only did my grammar improve, he taught me some memorable things in the boudoir."

According to my friend and colleague Bruce Fredenburg, *"women are definitely attracted to successful men. If they weren't, they'd be hanging out at the unemployment office, looking for men who are reading "I'm Ok, You're Ok!"*

It is evident that women love to feel a part of their man's world. So brush up on your conversational skills and intellectual savvy. Throw in a couple witty anecdotes and before you finish reading your current issue of Forbes Magazine, you'll be on top of things, and making the Dean's List all over again.

Women are also attracted to men who have a connection with other people. They are attracted to the gent who knows where's the action. Status then, is the most attractive trait.

Kimberly, 32, Lobbyist, Washington, D.C.

"I'm attracted to the guy who has the community connection. What I mean is the guy who knows everyone and what's going on in town."

Seduce Me!

Carol, 26, Hair Stylist, Hollywood, California

"Oh yeah, give me the guy who knows the action and he'll wake up in my bed every time!"

Women definitely find popularity to be a very desirable trait. This is because, if others like and trust you, she too will want to get to know you. Not to add that a connection with others proves that by no means are you a crazed lover.

Lastly, when a man is well connected, it leaves an impression of power. Oftentimes men are able to exploit these connections and rise to prominence. After all, power is the ultimate aphrodisiac.

What about looks? Just how important are looks to women? Of course physical prowess is important. Could anyone be so naive as to believe that looks don't matter to women? I'd like to point out that a women's definition of attraction is quite different from a man's.

We men are obsessed by a women's looks especially certain body parts. The list is endless, leg-man, butt-man, breast-man.... I myself was 30 before I realized that there was more to a woman than just her breasts.

Of course women are attracted to a man's anatomical attributes, yet they don't seem quite as preoccupied with looks as are men. Perhaps it's a throwback from our cave dwelling days. A time when men were sought for their abilities as providers.

Samantha, 34, Insurance Agent, San Francisco, California

"Looks are important. Yet for me, it's his appearance that truly matters. I look at a man's clothes. Especially his shoes. Fellas, badly kept shoes and Samantha no can do!!! After all, if he isn't detail oriented, how can he ever hope to please me... you do know what I mean?"

Patti, 25, Spokes model, Atlanta, Georgia

"I can't stand a guy who has no sense of style. Come on guys, it's the new millennium, get rid of the three- piece pin-stripe suit."

It is evident that women pay particular attention to the well coiffured man. Yet women don't want a prissy gent. What women want is a man who takes care of himself and is equally contemporary and upbeat. Yet the most prevalent quality I hear women stress over and over, is emotional availability.

Sherry, 29, Cocktail Waitress, Redondo Beach, California

"I am fortunate because I constantly meet new men. I must admit, I've heard every line imaginable. Yet I'm a push over for the confident, witty type. The biggest problem I have with the men that I meet is that they aren't emotionally available."

Dena, 27, Bartender, Chicago, Illinois

"Most of the men I meet are either married or involved. I guess that would classify as emotionally unavailable. I just don't permit myself to go down that road. After all, opening Pandora's Box would create a whole new set of complications in my life."

Is it true that so many men are emotionally unavailable? Men, whatever their reasoning, profess to be there for a woman with the one key exception, the committed relationship. Most men not only want their cake, they want to eat it as well. Men believe that if they set parameters in the beginning, the relationship will not get out of hand.

Gents, you are only kidding yourselves. When dealing with matters of the heart, reason simply cannot be applied. If you don't want to run the risk of a fatal attraction, think twice before professing your undying love just to get in her pants. If a woman truly wants you, she'll take whatever you are willing to give... for starters. Remember, women believe that they can change and mold you into what they want. If you are just looking for the flavor of the month, all hell will eventually break loose.

Let's recapitulate before moving on to the next chapter. We have learned in our quest to discover what women find irresistible in men, women are basically looking for the same qualities in men. These are:

- Success

- Status

- Looks/Appearance

- Emotional Availability

What about the " bad boy?" you ask. True, some women are definitely attracted to the "bad boy". They do indeed find him to be exciting and stimulating. However, women also believe that they can eventually mold him into the type they are looking for.

Martie, 32, Realtor, Scottsdale, Arizona

"Bad boys were always a part of my dating life. It took me awhile, but I finally realized that they eventually prove to be lousy providers. Who the hell would want a man like that?"

Kay, 26, Voice Coach, Burbank, California

"Touché... The bad boy who doesn't straighten out is nothing but a loser."

Now that we armed with the information to fulfill her subconscious needs, let's put it into practical application.

Seduce Me!

Chapter Two

Dress For Sex-Cess

"Image is everything."

Andrei Agassi

"A paradise of fools to few unknown."

John Milton

Now that we know what she wants in a man, how do we catch her eye? Just like the Nike commercial featuring tennis great, Andrei Agassi, "Image is everything."

It amazes me how out of step some men can be when it comes to contemporary fashion. This is not to say that you must religiously read GQ Magazine or hire a fashion consultant. What I will impress upon you is to develop a look that is uniquely you. A look that portrays who you are and what you are all about.

No man can attract every woman. However, when your clothing projects an image that is uniquely you; women who are attracted to that look, will certainly give you the once over. Think of today's hot celebrities, we always visualize them with a look that is unmistakably their own.

Women agree that whatever style a man chooses, he should look like he paid attention to what he's wearing. On the cautionary side, over fastidiousness sends up an alarm. Come now guys, fashion perfection will send out a signal that you're either gay, or an anal-retentive control freak. After all, your objective is to look dressed... not obsessed.

Leena, 28, Accountant, San Juan Capistrano, California

"I like a neat appearance. I don't like men who look like they are trying too hard."

Maggie, 26, Waitress, Denver, Colorado

"Definitely no designer names plastered across his chest. The ensemble look is a big no-no with me."

Katelin, 30, Spokes Model, Dallas, Texas

"I go for the casual look. Uptight loses my interest. Jeans or Khakis with a casual shirt catches my eye every time."

Whatever your look, it is imperative that your clothing fit properly and flatters your physique. Never wear clothes that are too baggy or too tight. And the ultimate no-no, don't show too much flesh. I don't care how well built you are. Add a couple of chains around the neck, and she'll be convinced that you are Guido from da' Bronx.

Shawna, 25, Model, New York City

"Guys should wear clothes that fit and flatter their physique. I hate it when a guy looks like he picked up his clothes at the second hand store. Vintage clothing is definitely not a part of my vocabulary."

Becca, 30, Bonds Analyst, Chicago, Illinois

"When a guy spends all of two minutes to get ready and go out, my first suspicion is did he even bathe?"

Cassandra, 32, Stock Broker, New York City

"An immediate turn-off is the guy who exposes too much flesh. He should look like my date, not a boy-toy that I bought and paid for."

I can't stress enough that if you want to score with women, you must first develop a look that is uniquely you, a look that women will also find appealing. Only in this way will you be dressed for sex-cess.

Still in doubt? Here's one sure way to develop your image. Ask a female friend to take you shopping. Let her advise you on what types of clothes work for you and what don't.

The beauty of this strategy is multi-facetted. Not only are you developing your image, you are learning what specifically attracts this woman. After all, if you are comfortable enough with her to ask her advice, perhaps you're overlooking a potentially hot relationship. Better still, she may be one of man's most fervent fantasies: A friend with benefits!

But I've digressed. We will discuss the "friend with benefits" relationship in a future chapter.

What is important is that you simply can't go wrong with advice of an attractive single woman.

Seduce Me!

Chapter Three

Do Pick Up Lines Work?

"I like to do all the talking myself.
It saves time and prevents arguments."

Oscar Wilde

"Good luck is something you create. Bad luck is
something you endure."

Walter Richard Hamilton

Do pick up lines work? The answer to this question is imperative for our success at the game of L'Amour. Without hesitation-no. Absolutely not! For the record I will emphatically state that pick up lines simply don't work.

Tanya, 28, Sales Representative, Phoenix, Arizona

"Pick up lines are a turn off. They are insincere and make me feel like a sex object."

Laini, 26, Secretary, Portland, Oregon

"I hate the guy with the cheesy lines. I'm not cheap so don't treat me that way."

Seduce Me!

Victoria, 31, Publicist, New York City

"I also hate the guy who compliments me on my looks. Come on guys, be more creative. There's more to me than just physical attributes."

Lorna, 25, Graduate Student, Santa Barbara, California

"I'm always flattered when a guy approaches me. However, what I'm looking to hear is sincerity. Anything else and it's.... bye, bye."

Gents, I must concur with our panel. Women want sincerity. Once she feels comfortable with the situation, she'll then be willing to strike up a conversation. At this point, you must be a good listener. In this way you will put her at ease and she'll begin to open up and relax.

Women prefer the direct approach. You'll have much better results if you walk up and simply introduce yourself.

I myself believe in the cautionary approach. I always try to make eye contact or get a smile. This doesn't mean that she's offering an invitation to her boudoir, so proceed with caution.

Why then do men insist on using pick up lines? This is obviously due to the difference between the way men and women think. As mentioned earlier, women prefer sincerity. Men believe that they must say something memorable to separate them from the pack.

I'm always amused when I hear one guy ask another what he thinks of this or that line. Stop and think about it, even if he likes what he hears, all you've done is impress another man. Special bulletin! This book is about seducing women. What matters is what impresses them.

The game plan is simple. Once you've introduced yourself, you need to move the conversation steadily passed, " who are you and what do you do?" In short, what you need is a conversation sparker. You need to move steadily from idle, chit-chat to that all consuming question... is he shag worthy?

Keep in mind that you must proceed with caution. During the obligatory " getting to know you" phrase, present yourself as a good listener. Not only will you put her at ease, she'll also feel that the two of you are making a connection. She will also enjoy the fact that you like hearing about her and her interests. Let's face it; we all enjoy talking about ourselves, especially when that person finds us attractive.

We have learned from our panel members to never compliment a woman on her looks. She will immediately see this as just another trite " come on." Worse yet, she'll conclude that you are just another loser trying to get into her pants.

Try complimenting her on her jewelry or accessories. After all, women love to shop. One could say that a little "shoptalk" goes a long way.

Be careful not to compliment her on the staples such as a suit, dress, shirt, or blouse. Women are no strangers to this approach so beware. Worse yet, since you want to discuss clothing you may convince her that you are gay. As comedian Jerry Seinfeld would say *"Not that there's anything wrong with that!"*

As I mentioned, jewelry and accessories are a safe way to steer the conversation. This is because for a woman accessorizing is an art. Realistically, an accessory is something that she added to catch eyes.

By complimenting her on her choice of accessories is in actuality praising her taste. This compliment goes much further than the standard: " I love your eyes." (As you gaze down at her breasts).

Jewelry can also be good to make headway. Oftentimes jewelry comes as a gift. A story will usually ensue, so here is your opportunity to capitalize on the situation. Sit patiently and be a good listener. Trust me, you'll definitely move one step closer to being shag worthy.

Once you are more experienced you can safely progress to complimenting her on subtleties in her attire. For example, a shade of color in her blouse that is meant to accentuate her attributes.

Try this for a conversation sparker: *"That shade of green really brings out the color of your eyes."*

Although I have had great success with this type of approach you may feel that it is not indicative of you and the image you are projecting. No problem... when in doubt, her shoes. Why? All women love shoes.

The successful approach has more to do with how its packaged and presented. Take advantage of your personality to exploit the situation. For example, if you are friendly and humorous, use this to your advantage.

Once, after charming a young lady at length about her good taste in shoes; I knew she was ready for more. In the interest of illustrating a point, permit me the liberty of editing the actual length of the conversation.

"With all this talk of shoes, I couldn't help but notice your ankles," I sighed playfully.

"My ankles?" Becca inquisitively glanced downward.

"Yes," I toyed with her. "They are.... So delicate."

"I've got to hand it to you," she smiled with subtle coquetry. *"You're scoring points."*

I gave her an inquiring glance. *"Really?"*

"I thought I've heard it all," she took a deep breath. *"But no one has ever complimented me for having delicate ankles."*

Let's stop right there. I know that some of my readers are excusing my flirtations as foolish. Perhaps, but all was done in fun and good taste. Then again, I scored. After all, doesn't the end justify the means?

I do want to emphasize a very powerful tool at our disposal... our voice. Most women are curious about a man's mouth.

Lynette, 34, Artist, Monterey, California

"I oftentimes find myself drifting off wondering what his lips will feel like when we kiss."

Haley, 28, Tax Preparer, Henderson, Nevada

"Since we're going there, I wonder what his mouth will feel like once he goes down on me."

Teresa, 25, Lingerie Model, Dallas, Texas

"Ditto on both comments!!!"

Since women are so obsessed with men's mouths, you need to capitalize on this romantic recourse. The experts that I interviewed also stress taking this obsession a step further.

Bruce Fredenburg, MFCC, Licensed Hypnotherapist

"Most of us don't realize how intoxicating our voices can be. Here are three steps to make your voice more alluring to women."

Step #1: Slightly lower your voice. Most women feel that the lower the voice, the manlier the man. This is because a deeper voice suggests reassurance. Women are often reminded of how their fathers took care of them.

Step #2: Speak in a subtle rhythmic tone. Don't hesitate to take full advantage of voice inflection on select words. For effect, try to always end your phrases on an upbeat note.

Step #3: Slow your speaking pace. Think about it. You are usually nervous upon first meeting a woman. Speaking slower will make you appear confident and patient. You will also help relax her and put her at ease.

A subdued voice will soon lead to her matching her breathing rhythm to yours. Once you have mastered these three steps, its time to take it a step further.

When chatting with women, try to steer the conversation to positive memories from her life. Research has proven that if you get someone talking about pleasantries of their past, they in turn, will associate those feelings with you.

Rhonda, 26, Stockbroker, New York City

"There's this guy I usually run into at the happy hour. He always made me feel good and forget my stressful day. One night, I took him home and it was great! Now when I need a pick me up, who do you think I call?"

Darla, 28, Copywriter, Denver, Colorado

"I went on a blind date. Though he was only of average looks, his voice captivated me. He got me thinking about my life and other things that I don't usually discuss on a first date. Not only was I feeling good, he held me spellbound. As he pulled up to my apartment, I leaned over and asked him what he wanted for breakfast."

Laura, 32, Editor, Chicago, Illinois

"I have a similar situation. There's this guy that I see... he can literally talk me out of my clothes."

The process of getting someone to recall positive experiences is known as Neurolinguistic Programming. " NLP," according to Bruce Fredenburg, author of "Women Good, Men Bad?" is a very positive approach to meeting people and having them recall you in a favorable light.

All I can say gents is fine-tune this skill. Once you do, she'll be squirming in her seat every time you say, " Remember...."

Seduce Me!

Chapter Four

Is She Just Playing You?

"There is no sin except stupidity."

Oscar Wilde

"Experience is the name everyone gives
to their mistakes."

Oscar Wilde

Only in our dreams do beautiful women fight among themselves to get us into their beds. How then do we know whether she really wants us or is just playing us for a sucker?

Let's start with drinks. I'm often amused by how some gents so flippantly buy drinks for women.

My female friends often tell me that even if they are broke, all they have to do is smile and some fool will keep them in drinks all night long.

I'm not saying it is wrong to buy a woman a drink. My point is that you should buy with discretion.

Whenever I make eye contact or make a connection with women, I always have the waitress ask her for permission to send over a drink. This will usually spark up a conversation. If you've been taking care of your waitress and tipping her accordingly, she's sure to say only wonderful things about you.

I would also caution you on running over to your belle dance for the obligatory thank you. Let the mystery build. If she smiles and indicates her pleasure, simply acknowledge her with a smile.

It is imperative for you to understand that the ball is in her court. If she is interested, she'll give you the subtle go ahead. She will do this by continuing to check you out and occasionally flashing a demure smile.

Most experts argue that the study of body language is a sure-fine guide to landing ladies in your bed. Allan Pease, author of *"Signals: How To Use Body Language for Power, Success and Love"* believes that it is imperative to learn how to decipher the more subtle and unconscious signals between people.

The biggest mistake most men make is that they either move too fast or they don't make a move at all. This is because the average male hasn't a clue when it comes to reading the unconscious cues women give when they are attracted to a man.

I do want to caution you on nonverbal communication. Body language simply is not a language. Particular cues can vary on individual or situational factors. In other words, you have to play it by ear.

Gabriel Ra'am, author of *"Men and Women Beyond Words,"* says that a behavior deemed universal by interested women is the tilting or turning of the head just enough to expose the neck. Ra'am also points out that when a woman reveals her palms or wrists that she is opening up.

Most of us have heard that if a woman plays with her hair, she's interested. This is particularly true if she pushes it away from her face. Better still, if she does this in a seductive manner.

Another sure-fire sign that she's interested is if she unconsciously spreads her legs. This is a little tougher to follow if you are both seated at a table. After all, should you drop down for a look, she's sure to notice. However, if she's standing and subtlety widens her stance, this is a good indication that she's warming up to you. Other "leg signs" include crossing them. She's definitely at ease with you when she crosses her legs and reveals a part of her thigh.

The classic indication in body language is the foot. If she slides her toes in and out of her shoe, things are definitely going your way. And if she slips out of her shoe and slides her foot up your thigh, holler for the check and take her back to your place!

The experts agree that body language is not an exact science. They also agree on one signal. When a couple starts to mirror each other, a connection is being made. When people show rapport with each other, they swivel their upper bodies toward each other and align their shoulders in parallel.

Once you get to this point in the conversation, the cues will become easier to read. We all know the obvious signs. If she touches you.... She's interested.

Now you are armed with a few clues to read her familiar cues. Make the most of them and hopefully the only question that you'll have to ask is, *"Your place or mine?"*

Seduce Me!

Chapter Five

The First Date

"Love is a battle not fought with bombs and bullets.
It is fought with flowers, candy, and jewelry."

"One thing about keeping your mouth shut,
no one can say you're wrong."
A very wise man

You've done your homework and diligently pursued her to spark interest. Now you've got to get her involved and score that date.

The worst thing that you can do is to not plan that all-important first date. The second thing that most men blow, is what I call *"the all or nothing attempt."* You are taking a big risk by asking out someone you know almost nothing about.

According to sexperts Louis and Coperland, you must realize the importance of the initial, priming dates. These dates are for lunch, a cup of coffee or someplace in public. These meetings are of the utmost importance. You need to learn enough about each other to pique some interest and see where it leads.

The importance of the priming date is to get a woman thinking romantically about you. Let's now take a look at some strategies to get you over the hurdle.

A priming date should always be at a location that is easy for both of you to find. Figure on spending a minimum of thirty minutes and no more than seventy- five minutes together. Your goal here is to keep her interested and wanting more.

Definitely let her know that you are interested and probe with questions to see if the feelings are mutual. RED FLAG! Don't push to hard or you'll push her off.

Continue to probe by complimenting her a couple of times and touch her a few times. These should be quick, non-intrusive touches. An example of this would be to lead her to her seat, and brush her arm. This will help make her comfortable with you. Gauge her reaction to ensure that she's not put off in any way.

Eye contact is not only important, it is essential. Men have a bad habit called the "wandering eye." Keep your focus on her and you'll definitely see the attention reciprocated.

Years ago I saw Warren Beatty on a television show. When asked why he was so successful with women, his answer was concise and most definite. Warren went on to tell the host that when he was in the company of a woman, he gave her his undivided attention. He made her feel like she's the only woman in the room.

Now think about that gents. Warren Beatty has probably dated more women than you could possibly imagine. Do you think he knows?... oh yeah!

Marguerite, 28, Clothing Buyer, Los Angeles, California

"I recently had lunch with a guy I met at a party. What turned me on was his attentiveness. I knew he wanted me and I became curious to get to know him."

Molly, 34, Columnist, Phoenix, Arizona

"Same thing happened to me. This guy was so sweet. I knew he was attracted to me by the way he eyed me."

Jackie, 27, Musician, Hollywood, California

"What I like about the guy I'm dating now is his patience. He really wanted to get to know me. We had coffee a couple of times and he asked questions about my career aspirations and my interests in general. He then came to the piano bar and enjoyed the show. We've been dating strong for eight months."

Along with attentiveness, it's of the utmost importance to remember TRUTH. Do women really want the truth? What they want is correct answers. I'll prove my point. "Honey, do I look fat in this dress?"

Another reason that I like the priming date, it affords us the opportunity to see whether there is potential. Up to this point, we've invested only minimal time, effort and money. Besides those innocent romps were light- hearted and fun.

The next step, however, is crucial to scoring. If you are going for seduction, you need to spend some quality time with her. You want to also make her feel like she's spent enough time with you without being a slut.

Four to five hours would be the maximum time for a first rendezvous. I caution you on too lengthy of a date. You still do not know each other well enough and you can always blow it.

You also want to plan the appropriate activity for the date. Pick a setting that she will enjoy.

Now that she's given you the go ahead, let's move to the preliminaries. As always, we want to make a good first impression.

Seduce Me!

Make sure you have your car washed. Remember, it's all about image and a dirty car drops you to slob category.

Celia, 24, Nurse, Santa Fe, New Mexico

"I went on a first date. This guy had a nice car, but it was filthy! I swear it looked like he lived in it. The worst part was when we arrived at the restaurant. Would you believe the loser pulled up to valet parking?"

Madison, 25, Web Designer, Seattle, Washington

"I've got you beat. I went on a first date and he hadn't even cleaned his junk away from the passenger seat. It took him fifteen minutes to decide where in the trunk everything should go."

Celia and Madison bring up an interesting point... a man's car. To most men their car is an expression of who they are and how they project themselves. A man's automobile is to him, what the house represents to a woman.

Gents, if you want to score points, don't just keep you car clean; keep it immaculate. Even if you aren't into cars, trust me on this one.

Is it imperative to always be driving a new car? Not necessarily. I believe it is important to make a statement with the car that you drive. And no, she will not be impressed with the bumper sticker that your other car is a Ferrari.

I love the classic roadster look. This is why I choose to drive a BMW Z-3 it is the perfect retro-sports car. To add to the image, my license plate says: *"SPDMON (SPEED DEMON), License to Thrill."* Just enough of the "bad boy" persona to entice.

I also drive an Alfa Romeo. My buddies, John Sherer and

Dan Goglanian and I, rebuilt a "Spider" for fun. Of course, it didn't hurt that my Uncle Al rebuilds and restores cars for a living.

What's next? I hope a Lotus Espirit. It would also be fun to get my nephew Austin, involved with the project.

Do you need to be as big a car enthusiast as myself? Of course not. I enjoy driving them and they are a good " ice breaker."

We've already discussed your appearance in chapter two, "Dress for Sex-Cess." The most important point that I'd like to reiterate is to take pride in your appearance. Show her that you are as equally excited about this date and went to lengths to impress her.

One of the things that men don't understand is the lengths a woman goes to so as to impress you on the date. Women take pride in their public appearance. They not only want to please you, they want to impress other women.

Della, 22, Receptionist, Anaheim, California

"I went on a first date with this guy in sales. Although he wore a suit and looked great, it was what he had been wearing all day. Since we were going to dinner, I wore a dress and had my hair and nails done. Big disappointment!"

Connie, 24, Dental Assistant, Long Beach, California

"I recently had a first date that I was very excited about. This guy was so cute and he was taking me to my favorite seafood restaurant in the marina. I went out and bought a new dress and shoes to match. You won't believe what he wore. He had on a tacky Hawaiian shirt, cargo pants, and sandals. I was so embarrassed, after all, this is where I hang out."

Seduce Me!

Angie, 23, Secretary, Salt Lake City, Utah

"You don't know the meaning of embarrassed. I went on a first date to a very elegant restaurant. I dressed appropriately but my date, an accountant, sure didn't. He said that since he wore a suit at work, he preferred to dress down in the evening. That's fine, but he should have taken me to a place with a relaxed atmosphere. He wore a cotton blazer and corduroy slacks. The worst part was the T-shirt. It was one of those with the tie drawn on it. What a loser!!!"

The most important thing is dress appropriately to wherever it is that you are going. I'll say it again; you never get a second chance to make a good first impression.

I realize that there are no hard fast rules in dating. You have to improvise to impress the woman that you are with. The safest route is to plan the date and take her to some place that she will enjoy. She's not a fool. You'll score points because you went out of your way for her to have a good time.

So do we go to the extra effort? Should you bring flowers or any other gift? The answer is yes and no. The key is the woman. Flowers or a gift may impress her, however, to some women, they may feel that you are moving to fast.

This is why I encourage the priming dates. You get a better idea of who she is and what she's all about.

Something else to take into consideration. If you are meeting somewhere, what will she do with flowers on the date?

Sophie, 28, Publicist, Los Angeles, California

"I went out on a first date with this cute restauranteur. He bought one long stem, yellow rose. I loved it! What I really liked he remembered that yellow is my favorite color."

Carmen, 25, Office Manager, Denver, Colorado

"I had the exact opposite experience. This fellow was a sommelier. He may know wine, but he sure doesn't know women. On the surface, the date was perfect. He bought me a dozen roses and we had an excellent dinner. We then went to an intimate little bistro where we sampled several wines. I did realize that he didn't care for me. It was all part of his game plan to seduce me. I don't know who he went home with that night, but it wasn't me."

Rosemary, 21, Paralegal, Brea, California

"I love gifts and I'll take anything that my dates want to buy me."

Heather, 25, Pharmaceutical Sales, Tucson, Arizona

"I actually don't like it. I feel like he's moving too fast. Slow down and just get to know me. Once you do, then the appropriate gift is most appreciated."

Paula, 27, Film Editor, Studio City, California

"I just feel like it's a contrived move. The first date is about getting to know each other and deciding if there should be a second date."

Brenda, 25, Court Reporter, Dallas, Texas

"I like receiving flowers on a first date. For me, it's part of the dating ritual. It shows that he has class. I especially look for manners. I won't tolerate a harsh man."

Brenda brings up a very interesting point in dating etiquette. Most men claim that with the advent of "Women's Lib," they aren't sure how to act. I've heard every excuse for not opening a door or pulling out a woman's chair. My beliefs are quite simple. Good manners are just that. There is absolutely nothing wrong with opening a door for someone, regardless of gender.

Seduce Me!

If you are looking for the proverbial " Rule of Thumb," there is none. Marriage and Family Therapist, Louise Tenbrook Whiting, shared an interesting story with me regarding the origins of this tale.

"The Rule of Thumb" has been attributed to British Common Law. It was believed, when disciplining a wife, men could beat their women with a rod. Yet to be just, husbands had to ensure that it's width was no larger round than that of their thumb. Eliminate this phrase from your vocabulary."

Whether or not you decide to give the extra effort and bring a gift, it is important that you are polite and show good manners. For me, this is nothing more than giving respect.

Who should pay for what you ask? A recent survey of singles concludes by seventy-three percent that the man should pay for the first date.

While on a date, I find a woman's "paying" behavior most interesting. I am referring to the use of money and how women view it.

Oftentimes a woman offers to pay or go "Dutch," it's a test. She's curious to see just how cheap you are. Gents... beware! It may be a cheap night out but you'll surely end up sleeping alone.

Up to this point, our first date has been moving steadily along and you both are comfortable with each other. Proceed with caution. Let the "real you" out a little at a time. You'll never score with her by arguing or through competition. This is a date, not a debate.

Kristen, 26, Corporate Recruiter, San Jose, California

"I was on a first date and everything was fine. He was polite and a good listener. We enjoyed a quiet dinner and decided to drive into San Francisco. As we passed Pac Bell Stadium, he

proceeded to show off his knowledge of the Giants. I disagreed with some of his statistical information and the real him came out. Rather than accept that I too was an avid Giants fan, he figured I was just a girl and didn't know a thing. Too bad for him that I'd never date him again. My company has season tickets and I'm in change of their dispersal."

Tina, 28, Event Planner, Houston, Texas

"My date went from prince to toad while we were playing darts. I beat him two out of tree games and he immediately became agitated. He cut the evening short and took me home. Oh, well... his loss."

Liz, 24, Actress, Burbank, California

"What attracted me to my boyfriend is that he doesn't feel he has to outdo me. If I know, or can do something that he can't, he never hesitates to ask for help. My ex-boyfriend was the exact opposite. To him, everything was a competition."

Over the years, my male friends have asked why I do so well with women. One reason for sure, I don't compete with them. It's bad enough that we men compete over women. It's foolish to extend such behavior to our date. Perhaps most of us have no common sense. My friend, and motivational speaker, Zig Ziglar, is quick to point out that *"common sense just ain't common."*

I can't caution you enough to tread softly when sharing your opinions and beliefs. A first date is not conducive to an opinionated, one-sided conversation.

Oftentimes, at dinner, men get a little too comfortable. This usually occurs because they are drinking more than advisable. Your date can immediately turn around if alcohol starts doing the talking.

Seduce Me!

Rachel, 31, Property Manager, San Diego, California

"Since it's a first date, I'm careful not to get piled with alcohol. My date can surely do the same. Giving a goodnight kiss to a slobbering drunk isn't my idea of attractive.

Holly, 37, Graphic Designer, Portland, Oregon

"It's amazing how obnoxious some men get when they drink. Especially when they realize that they are not scoring with me. There have been a couple of guys that I refuse to get into their car. Thank God for taxi- cabs!"

Susan, 21, Secretary, Huntington Beach, California

"Having just turned twenty-one, drinking is a big deal. Slamming shots is not my idea of a romantic date."

Cammie, 25, Kindergarten Teacher, Tulsa, Oklahoma

"If he's driving, he's not drinking. It's my rule. I also respect that decision so I won't drink either. Besides, it's a first date and we should be on our best behavior."

My best advise is don't try too hard. Let the connection between the two of you develop.

A recent survey conducted by NBC's popular television show, "The Other Half," polled women as to what appealed to them while on a date:

- Women want a man who is a good listener

- They want a polite man with manners

- Women also look for shared values

- Intelligence is very important

- A sense of humor is a must

When the same audience was polled as to what was an immediate turn off, they gave us the following answers:

- Lack of intelligence

- No sense of humor

- Unemployment

One last dinner tip. Try to eat a light meal. It is much easier to digest and help to keep you alert. Afterall, should you get lucky, it's pretty tough to perform like a sexual athlete after a tri-tip.

The end of the evening is drawing near and you've shown her a good time. Assuming that you've done everything correctly, it's time to move in for the close...

Don't rush in or push too hard or you'll blow it. Here's where the date will either come to an end or she'll be asking, *"How do you want your eggs in the morning?"*

Seduce Me!

Chapter Six

Seduce Her

*"Fortune favors the brave and those
who learn by their mistakes."*
Old Spanish Proverb

*"Women need a reason to have sex.
Men just need a place."*
Billy Crystal

*"Masturbation is having sex with
someone that you love."*
Woody Allen

You're on her doorstep and it's time to make your move. What next? If you've been paying attention all evening, you picked up on all of the subtle cues she gave you.

Never ask to kiss her. Here's where she wants a man not a wimp!

Sandra, 29, Public Relations, New Orleans, Louisiana

"A guy once asked if he could kiss me. I couldn't help it, but I broke into a laughter. High school was a long time ago."

55

Seduce Me!

Janet, 27, Meeting Planner, Miami, Florida

"This guy asked me if he could kiss me good-night and it just blew the mood. The allure was gone, I just smiled and offered my hand."

Most men are just afraid of being rejected. Yet you'll never know what she'll say until you try. Here's a little statistical information that might help to put you at ease. A recent survey conducted by "Society" magazine asked:

"How many women have had sex on a first date?"

- *67% of women had sex on a first date*

- *21% have done so more than once*

- *7% have done so more than ten times*

Armed with our new found information, it's time to make your move. What is important about your first kiss is that it must be all that you are.

Again, if you've been paying attention to the cues she's been giving you, you'll know just how she wants to be kissed.

Pamela, 31, Chef, Long Beach, California

"My date moved in to kiss me. Just as I parted my lips, a huge tongue darted toward me. The kiss was terrible and I sent him on his way."

Jody, 26, Horse Trainer, Santa Ynez, California

"This guy drew me in and kissed me so hard that I thought I was in a wrestling match. Needless to say, he lost me on a TKO."

Robin, 25, Esthetician, Fort Collins, Colorado

"I had a date who was all teeth. He even wanted to bite my lip! All I could say was back off and get a grip."

Allison, 29, Nurse, Madison, Wisconsin

"My boyfriend knows how to kiss. He moved in slowly and gently explored my lips. As I responded, he kissed me deeper and deeper until I let myself go."

Dana, 30, Dentist, Trenton, New Jersey

"My boyfriend also knows how to kiss. Not only is he gentle, he caresses my neck until I am putty in his hands."

Clara, 24, Decorator, Santa Barbara, California

"On a recent date I practically mauled the guy I was with. He had the most kissable lips that I couldn't resist. He knew just how to kiss and caress me. After twenty minutes of necking, we were off to the bedroom."

Women's biggest reservation with first-time sex is nervousness. Everything from your apartment's decor to how good dinner was to her irrational fear that you'll think her butt is too big. All those variables play an important part in her dropping her drawers.

Something else that men should understand, women also experience peer pressure. Her girlfriends will be quick to ask if you are "boyfriend material." That's woman talk for is he "shagworthy?" She'll definitely think twice before she let's you round her bases and score. After all, she must defend her borderline sluttiness to her friends.

It is imperative to remember these points. At the end of the date, should your sure thing surprise you and switch gears, don't fret. Be patient. Reassure her that she's special and end the date gracefully.

You could foolishly push your honey and risk losing her altogether. "No means "NO," so don't blow it.

Women expect you to give it the old college try. All is not lost; it's just the end of round one.

According to Tracey Cox, author of "Hot sex: How To Do It," women are more comfortable when a man tries to bed her after three to six dates. By that many times she's thinking, *"Hey, why hasn't he made a move yet? Isn't he attracted to me?"* And asking her if it's too soon, reassures her that you think she's special enough to wait for, Cox says. *"Play it right and the answer should be, let's do it right here!"*

Chapter Seven

Dating Younger Women

"You only live once, but it does help if you get to be young twice."

George Burns

"An inordinate passion for pleasure is the secret for remaining young."

Oscar Wilde

"It's better to regret something you did rather than something you didn't."

Errol Flynn

After six years of marriage, I found myself single. Since it was I who had filed for divorce, I was eager to get on with my life. Since it had been some time that I had played the dating scene, I hardly knew what to expect.

The first woman I dated was ten years my junior. All things considered, ten years isn't that much nor was the gap between us. We had a great deal in common and enjoyed each other's company. The problem was that it was the wrong time for both of us. We had just left our spouses respectively and we needed time alone. Time again to rediscover who we were and where we wanted our lives to end up.

Seduce Me!

My second relationship was once again with a wonderful woman. However this time fifteen years separated us. Although we were both adults, fifteen years can be perceived as a bit much.

After the relationship had run its course, I once again found myself unattached. To my dismay, a young lady of twenty-one asked me out.

She worked for the BMW dealership where I serviced my Z-3 Roadster. She professed that she had a crush on me, but I was always involved.

After discussing my predicament with my friends, they all agreed that this was foolish. Did I heed their advice? Of course not! A twenty-one year old hard body wanted me, so why wouldn't I want her?

I kept our first date simple, lunch very near the dealership. I figured this would eliminate the awkwardness of ending a first date.

I was overwhelmed and to my surprise we had an exceptional time. We immediately made plans for the weekend... dinner in the marina.

I did feel somewhat awkward when I picked her up at her apartment. She had two roommates who also worked part-time and went to college. I guess I was just being foolish, as her girlfriends really seemed to like me.

After dinner, we had a romantic walk along the beach. Eventually we found ourselves back at my place.

I'll never forget that first night we were alone. Her innocence was intoxicating. Beautiful and alluring, she held nothing back and loved me with the singleness of mind and body....

Jamie, 26, Photographer, Boston, Massachusetts

"I like dating older guys. They treat me right and don't play games. My last boyfriend was twelve years older."

Carol, 27, Architect, Dayton, Ohio

"I'm really into my career. I guess I want to prove myself. Guys my age are still players. All they think about is scoring. The oldest guy I dated was eighteen years my senior."

Rikki, 24, Computer Sales, San Jose, California

"Guys my age are notorious for coming over with a video and a six pack thinking that they are going to spend the night. I've only dated one older guy. He was thirty-two. We were together for six months and it was great! Guys over thirty, call me."

Dating younger women does bring up some obvious concerns as well as some broad generalizations.

The immediate concern is obvious. Is she playing you for the money?

A woman, regardless of her age can always work you for the dough. Just because she's younger doesn't mean that she has an ulterior motive.

My own experiences would certainly prove to contrary, I have found that younger women are less concerned with fine dining and dancing.

Another plus when dating a younger woman; they usually don't have children. I don't have anything against kids, however, I like the freedom of leaving for the weekend.

I live at the beach in Santa Barbara, California and I have two sports cars. It's almost a weekend ritual to drop the top on my

Z-3 Roadster or ALFA Romeo and cruise up the coast. To put it bluntly, women with children simply don't have that luxury with their time.

It seems that the critics of dating younger women are usually those women who are middle-aged and stuck at home.

I definitely do not want anyone to think I'm criticizing middle-aged women. All I'm saying is for various reasons they have a different agenda than mine. I am more than willing to respect their views as I hope they will show me the same courtesy.

I spoke with several men on the issue of dating women younger than themselves. Their biggest concern seemed to be, *would younger women date them due to the age gap?*

Felicia, 34, Attorney, Richmond, Virginia

"I put my ex-husband through law school. Once he landed a lucrative position with a prestigious firm, he filed for divorce. I went back to school and now I practice law. I love dating men ten to twenty years my senior. What about the age gap you ask? Bull! People either share common interest or they don't. It's simply a fallacy to believe otherwise."

Melanie, 30, Engineer, Renton, Washington

"I love men in their forties. They are much more settled. I think it's because they're usually divorced and have learned from their mistakes."

Christine, 28, High School Teacher, Chino Hills, California

"I love dating guys ten to fifteen years older. They seem to have time for me. Younger guys always want to party."

Candy, 25, Hair Stylist, Memphis, Tennessee

"Not only do younger guys want to party, they usually have roommates. Put a bunch of guys together and it's sports, beer, chicks- party! Now I date men at least ten years older."

Wanda, 27, Sound Editor, Hollywood, California

"Girls, fast cars, nightlife, girls, reckless romance and girls. That's what I think most young guys are into. The past two years I've been dating older men exclusively. The best of the lot had twenty years on me."

Another point that is usually brought up concerning older men dating younger women, the "Father-figure syndrome." Critics are usually convinced that she wants a "surrogate daddy" to replace a relationship that she never had with her own father. Of course this does happen in the real world. I do believe that there are a multitude of reasons why younger women are attracted to older men.

Veronica, 29, Flight Attendant, Los Angeles, California

"I get tired of the game playing with younger guys. Currently I'm dating a man who is forty-two. We have a great time together. We really enjoy each others company. He's so patient with me. What I like is he's never jealous. I travel a lot because that's my job. I don't have a guy at my every stop over and I'm certainly not out whoring in every club. Believe me, I've been accused of worse. My current beau is the exact opposite. Every homecoming he plans a special evening to celebrate my return. My father and I get along and he approves of my relationship.

Jenny, 26, Nurse, San Pedro, California

"I had the same problem. I work on a cruise ship. My past boyfriend just assumed I was partying in Cabo San Lucas or

sleeping with passengers. I think they've been watching too many porno flicks. Now my forty-seven year old boyfriend greets me at the door with flowers. Better still, mom and pop approve."

Gwen, 23, School Teacher, Lexington, Kentucky

"My guy is forty-five and I'm crazy for him. It turns me on to know that I excite him more than his past lovers. So much for wisdom with age- ha! He's always there for me and encourages me to pursue all that life has to offer. Need I say more?"

Earlier, I commented on the fact that I didn't particularly care to date women with children. How then do younger women feel about dating older men with children?

Nina, 24, Party and Event Planner, Detroit, Michigan

"My guy is thirty-seven. He's been divorced for three years and has a six year old daughter. At first, I didn't quite know how to react. Actually I've never been in that situation before. I will say this, I'm beginning to see what type of mother I'll make."

Judy, 28, Reporter, Falls Church, Virginia

"My boyfriend is forty-two. He's been divorced for twelve years. He has a sixteen year old son and a fourteen year old daughter. He sees them every other weekend. The magazine I write for constantly has me on the road. He's in television, a producer in Washington, D.C. It's difficult with schedules and families, but we make time for each other. I get along with his children. I attribute this to one simple rule. I interact with them as a friend, not their mother."

Julia, 27, Ski Instructor, Vail, Colorado

"I'm not dating any one man in particular. I do prefer older men, less head games. Some have had kids, but I've never met any of them."

Sarah, 29, Chiropractor, Carlsbad, California

"I'm engaged to a gentleman fourteen years my senior. He has a twelve year old daughter. We have a great relationship and she's always asking if we plan to start a family right away. She wants a baby sister. At least I won't have to worry about a babysitter."

Shari, 25, Piano Teacher, New York City, New York

"My guy is eleven years older. He has two boys. Their ages are six and four. He gets them every other weekend. I've never met them because I have only dated him for three months. Should our relationship continue to grow, helping to raise someone else's children is a big responsibility. I realize that I cannot look lightly upon my situation."

Karen, 30, Dentist, La Jolla, California

"My fiancée is forty-four. He's a doctor and a single parent. With his schedule, I know that I'll spend a great deal of time with his eight year old son. I gave it a great deal of thought and I not only love his son, I'm ready to accept the responsibility of a ready-made family."

I do not believe that age has a monopoly on responsibility. It's simply an individual matter. Where someone is in their life, the depth of their relationship and where they want to go from there.

Probably the number one red flag according to the critics of dating younger woman, the "Sugar Daddy." Is she working you for your money? Perhaps, however a women your age is just as capable of loving you for your wallet.

Yvonne, 23, Model, Los Angles, California

"When I first told my friends I was dating a man seventeen years older, they couldn't believe it. They just assumed that he was my sugar daddy. Although he's a successful commercial realtor, I make more money. I like him because he's kind, attractive, funny, and of course, great in bed!"

Marcy, 26, Tennis Instructor, Santa Monica, California

"My fella is twenty-one years older. When I told my parents, they threw a fit. I figured that it was no one's business but mine. When I didn't make it on the tennis circuit, I knew that I had no desire to return to Oldman, Florida. I then landed this job at a prestigious tennis club. Shortly there after I started dating. Most of the guys were players... you know what I mean. Then I met my guy. He's an art dealer. In the last year I've learned to appreciate art and his backhand has certainly improved.

Gents, we've now seen that young women from all walks of life can be and are attracted to older men. Before you run and make a pass at the first young chick you meet... beware! There are some basic discretionary guidelines to follow.

My own experience has taught me to never make the first move with a younger woman. Stop and think for a moment. If she has never been propositioned by an older man, she could very easily be frightened away.

I have my own sense of a chivalric code. For me, it is imperative that she know the score.

What do I mean? First, she must be experienced at L'amour.

More importantly, she must have also had her share of affairs of the heart.

Avoiding future complications is a must. Make sure that your young coquette knows the score and is up for a good time. Regardless of how experienced she may appear on the surface, is she still a "Babe in Toyland"?

If she's up for a few weeks of fun-filled frolic... enjoy. If she's hoping that the relationship will go to the next level and that is not your intent, you're open to problems. Only the worst possible ramifications can possibly occur.

A couple of years ago I was involved with a gorgeous young woman of twenty-four. She was literally a dream come true. It was the perfect affair, or so I thought. Complications began when she fell in love with me. For her, it was true love and she wanted to build a life together.

Unfortunately, I did not share her sentiments. I was in love with a fantasy of a beautiful swim-suit model who was head over heels in love with me.

Love hurts when only one is in love. It ended the only way it could. She walked away broken-hearted, never willing to see me again...

Paying attention to the subtle cues that women give is the key to seduction. Your belle dance is not different. Be observant and if she is interested, she will let you know how and when to seduce her.

On a lighter note; my friend Bobby Layton, simplifies the issue of dating younger women.

"If she can name all four of the Beatles, she's the best by me!!"

Seduce Me!

Chapter Eight

Dating Older Women

"If prefer women with a past. They're so damned amusing to talk to."

Oscar Wilde

"Strong women give big hickeys."

Madonna

After a threesome, an affair with an older woman is probably every young man's fantasy. I myself was thirty-four before I stopped dating older women. I enjoyed my relationships so much that I dated women my senior, almost exclusively.

While a high school junior, I began dating seniors. As a senior, I dated girls who were in college. Why, you ask? Most men believe that older women are more experienced and more willing to put out.

All I can say is that older women have always played a big part in my sexual escapades. I hope that you too will enjoy dating older women. Not only do they have a certain *je ne se quas*, you can damn well learn a lot.

What is it about younger men that attracts an older woman?

Connie, 44, Attorney, Bel Air, California

"I work a lot. Sometimes I forget that I have a life outside of practicing law. I dated a guy who was twenty-eight. That was two years ago. He brought the fun back into my life. The relationship fizzled after about eight months. I must admit, since then I've only dated younger guys."

Josie, 47, Office Manager, Tucson, Arizona

"The best thing about a younger man is trainability. I've dated guys as much as twenty years younger. Age simply doesn't matter to me. What I look for in a man is, 'Can I mold him into what I want?' If so, I'll definitely make it worth his while."

Susan, 57, Restauranteur, Baton Rouge, Louisiana

"Sex!!!"

Kathryn, 34, Secretary, Miami, Florida

"I'll also go with sex. It seems that younger men just have a higher sex drive. Right out of college is the best. They are like hungry young lions."

Pam, 41, Interior Decorator, Del Mar, California

"Don't forget stamina. They can go all night long. What they lack in technique, I can teach them."

Megan, 48, Jeweler, Boise, Idaho

"Young men like to go places and do things. Men my age and older are more settled. They are less adventurous and not as willing to try new things."

The obvious plus of having a liaison with an older women is evident. An older woman usually is sexually more experienced.

To add to her allure, she's usually less inhibited and more inclined to hedonism.

Now what could be better than a woman who is into sexual pleasure and has her eye on you?

The list goes on.. she usually has her own place and established in her career. She is not only willing to teach you, she's also willing to dress you. Gifts can abound as do weekend jaunts out of town.

Enjoy, enjoy, enjoy.... However, don't get consumed by your affair. Learn from her and grow.

I fondly recall a long term relationship that I had with a woman six years my senior. In short.. it was FABULOUS!!! Yet I would be the first to caution you on any spring/ autumn pairing.

Whatever happens, regardless how great the sex may be, do not permit yourself to fall in love with an older woman. Even if the relationship appears carefree, it's subject to a mass of complications down the road.

To begin with, an older woman is probably already set in her ways. You, by contrast, are looking for your identity.

An older woman knows what she wants and knows what it will take to meet her likes and needs.

Once you begin asserting your own goals for a definition of self, she'll usually conclude that it's time to move on and be done with you.

For the ambitious young lion, this can be tragic. Men typically define who they are by what they do, and how successful they are at their craft.

It's clear that being in love with an older woman will be the opening of Pandora's box. A multitude of hardships can ensue.

It's important to remember that she's been around and knows the score. You, on the other hand, are naive and in many cases, just a boy-toy.

The only thing worse than you falling in love with her, is if she also falls in love with you. The list of potential problems is endless.

What if down the road you want children and she has fulfilled her maternal desires. Worse yet, what if she can no longer have children? What if she already has children? Are you prepared to accept the responsibilities of fatherhood and a ready made family?

It takes a special couple who share a special love for each other to last a lifetime. Such a complicated affaire of the heart seems doomed and destined for failure.

It's best to take the relationship for what it is. An affair. Learn from her and most of all, enjoy this brief rendezvous. It is a moment in time that you captured together. It is your moment.... Live it to the fullest.

Part Two

Where To Meet Women

Chapter Nine

The Best Place To Meet Women

"Expect the unexpected or you won't find it."
Heraclitus

"Days are for sleep, nights are for play!"
Casanova

Where is the best place to meet women? I'm asked this question more than any other. The answer is quite simple, everywhere. If you seriously want to meet women you should be willing to exploit every opportunity.

I constantly advise men to say hello to every woman they come in contact with. Take a look at their reaction. Any opportunity? Remember, should a woman make eye contact, why not attempt a conversation and see where it goes.

I'm amused when men tell me that they can't deal with all that rejection. Stop worrying about embarrassment. It's not like she's apt to remember that three months earlier you made a pass at her. And since then, she's alerted the media claiming you to be a buffoon.

Remember William Smith? Of course you don't. However, Captain William J. Smith was the captain of the Titanic.

Seduce Me!

As long as the encounter was innocent and you conducted yourself as a gentleman, she probably found you flattering. Stop worrying about rejection and start saying "hi".

Let's take a look at some of the places you are apt to have better luck. Some of these locations have been typically identified as hot spots to meet women, while I'll surprise you with some others.

The Gym- We've been hearing about scoring at health clubs since the seventies. Why? Who doesn't want to sleep with hard bodies? Working out can produce many more prospects than you imagine. Most clubs have a juice bar and the members love to socialize after a workout.

Olivia, 30, Realtor, Pasadena, California

"I like meeting men at the gym. It's a fun environment and I get to see what they're packing."

Janet, 28, Photographer, Seattle, Washington

"Where else can I strut my stuff and get so much attention. Besides, I like a man who takes care of himself."

Keep in mind that health clubs usually have aerobics classes which women love. If you're a bit more daring, try the yoga class. Yoga is a discipline that's almost exclusively popular with women. Perhaps it's not macho enough for most men. Let me remind you, why are we at the gym? Besides, Tantric sex is phenomenal.

Lastly, if you are at that age where everything is starting to hang out, spread out or fall out; perhaps going to a health club wouldn't hurt at all.

The Supermarket- Stay away from grocery shopping during the day. Supermarkets are usually flooded with married women. We definitely do not want to go there, at least not in this book.

I like to go shortly after work. Look for women carrying a basket or shopping for one. After all, no one likes to eat alone.

Cynthia, 32, Optician, Topeka, Kansas

"I once met a guy at the grocery store. He told me that he didn't like eating dinner alone and would I join him for dinner? It was fun and we ended up dating for a few months."

After interviewing several women employees from grocery store chains, I learned of the ice cream aisle. It seems that frustrated women frequent this section later in the evening. Between eight and ten is a good time.

Jessica, 26, Secretary, Tempe, Arizona

"I wish more men knew about the ice cream aisle. When you are by yourself, whip cream isn't fun. It's just messy."

Deirdre, 31, Travel Agent, Memphis, Tennessee

"I so agree. Men need to know about the ice cream section. The times I've been lonely and dashed off for a pint, no luck. All I've ever found is caramel pecan and way too many calories."

Natalie, 22, Chorus Dancer, Las Vegas, Nevada

"If I could meet a man in the ice cream section, it would be wonderful! Just think of the fun, chocolate syrup, whip cream, strawberries...."

Well gents, there you have it. It's the ice cream aisle or bust.

Seduce Me!

The women are there. With a bit of luck, and a dash of panache, you too could be enjoying the flavor of the week.

Shoe Store- What do most women love to buy? You know it.... Shoes. Where should you be? Shoe department, where else!

Phyllis, 27, Dental Hygienist, Salt Lake City, Utah

"I once met a man while buying shoes. He was charming, fun and attentive. I must admit, I went home with him."

Brenda, 28, Loan Consultant, Columbus, Ohio

"I love shoes! If a guy has the patience to shop with me, I'll definitely make it worth his time."

Beauty Products Store- Nowadays it's more popular for men to care for their skin and hair. When you are out and about, drop into a beauty store. Women love to give advice on products.

Peggy, 34, Bank Teller, Pittsburgh, Pennsylvania

"I once met a guy when I was buying some beauty products. He asked me about hair color. After some colorful chit chat, his hair wasn't all I did!"

Samantha, 29, Esthetician, Olympia, Washington

"I love a man who takes the extra time to care for his skin. I do have a rule about dating clients. I hate to admit it, I've been picked up at the beauty supply store."

I'd also like to add another place along the same vein where I've had very good luck. The hair salon. My hair stylist constantly fixes me up. I love it! I've also been known to date a few hair dressers in my time.

Sporting Events- The best activities for meeting women are tennis and equestrian events. Women abound. Since I both ride and play tennis, it's easy to pursue a date. I will caution you on being too competitive with women. Remember, it's not the winning, it is about getting laid. I myself attribute my success with women simply because I don't compete with them.

Sarah, 25, Loan Processor, Scottsdale, Arizona

"I love horses. Especially Arabians. They are so beautifully exotic. I used to compete when I was in my teens. For me, if he doesn't like to ride horses, he'll never ride me."

Yvonne, 29, Telecommunications, Del Mar, California

"Riding is like foreplay. If he wants to mount me, he better know how to sit on a horse."

Sophie, 30, Graphic Designer, Fort Collins, Colorado

"If he can handle a horse, he's my type of man. Giddy up!!"

Sandy, 29, Insurance Sales, Akron, Ohio

"Tennis is my game. When I'm at the club, you can rest assured that I'm either playing with a friend or a client. Not only am I open to picking up a match here and there, I can be picked up. Sharpen your backhand if you want a date with me."

Michelle, 26, Stenographer, West Palm, Florida

"Set, match, love... that's my motto."

Seduce Me!

Lingerie Boutique – I've also found the lingerie boutique to be a great place to meet women. Think about it gents, beautiful women are modeling underwear for you. What else could possibly be better?

Lucy, 23, Lingerie Model, San Francisco, California

"Most of the men I meet are from restaurant shows that we do. I get at least twenty business cards each time. If the guy I call shows me a good time, I'll give him a second look at my undies."

Emily, 27, Customer Service Rep, Madison, Wisconsin

"I was once at a luncheon that included a lingerie show. This guy, who was seated at the next table was a real cutie. We constantly flirted back and forth. Finally he leaned over and whispered that he would like to see me in the lingerie being shown. Needless to say, he bought it for me. Later that evening, I gave him a private show."

Tina, 21, Lingerie Model, Portland, Oregon

"A guy once came into a boutique and asked for a private showing. The girl he was buying for sounded suspiciously like me. He then told me to pick something out that I'd like my boyfriend to buy for me. I informed him that I wasn't dating anyone. He smiled and said ' You are now.' We've been having a torrid affair for the last three months."

Weddings- This is probably one of the best places to meet available chicks. For women, it's awkward being single at a wedding. Most of the guests are discussing marriage. Worse yet, old friends keep asking why she hasn't found a husband.

SPECIAL BULLETIN! She's dressed to the tens and feeling a little insecure. The meal and the booze are free. What more could you ask for? Since you are in a tux, throw your best Bond-esque swagger and escort her out onto the dance floor. Your mission is to charm her right out of her gown and take her on the honeymoon weekend, without the wedding of course. The only question should be, are you up to accepting the mission?

Viveca, 30, Paralegal, Omaha, Nebraska

"I dreaded my best friend's recent wedding. Oh, I was happy for her. It's just that of all our friends, I was now the only one who remained single. I met this guy after the ceremony. He charmed me out onto the dance floor and later that evening, right out of my gown. It only lasted a few weeks, but it was blissful..."

Frankie, 28, File Clerk, Cranston, Rhode Island

"I'm the old maid of the group. I've met a man at every one of my girlfriend's weddings. I may not be married, but I sure am having fun."

When I was studying Chinese in Taiwan, my fellow classmates and I were notorious wedding crashers. Every weekend we would frequent the hotels in search of a wedding party and of course, the bridesmaids.

Taking special care to fill the "congratulatory red envelope" with the appropriate amount of money, we were the hit of Taipei. And just for a little extra fun, I always listed us as friends of the bride.

The Airport- These days, due to all of the security measures, it's a must to get to the airport earlier than ever before. It still gets worse. The lines are longer and the security checks are endless. Since it's impossible to change the situation, how then can we capitalize on our added delays? Simple... take the opportunity to meet new women.

Seduce Me!

Several factors need to be taken into careful consideration. First and foremost, make sure she's traveling alone. Imagine your dismay if some 6'5" hulk decides to use you for a floatation device.

While on patrol, be sure to note if she's new in town. Lost and lonely, or on a layover. Pending on her situation, you can then plan your approach. Make sure you fully assess her dilemma as it is key to your success.

If she's calling hotels, its fair to assume that she's new in town. Here's your chance to offer your help. A traveler in a strange town will appreciate a little kindness and especially a gentleman who's come to her aid.

If she doesn't know anyone in town, offer to take her to dinner. Even if she has local friends, still ask her out. After all, you've come to her aid and her friends undoubtedly have left her to fend for herself.

Tammy, 25, Secretary, Irvine, California

"When I first moved here from Sacramento, I met a guy at the airport. He was such a gentleman and ever so helpful. He carried my bags and took me to dinner. We had so much fun that I took him back to my new apartment. We actually ended up dating for two months and through him, I got to know Orange County and made new friends."

Lorelei, 35, Journalist, San Diego, California

"A few months ago, I was on assignment in San Francisco. After several delays and a rough flight, we landed almost three hours behind schedule. While picking up my luggage, I began chatting with a gorgeous gentleman. After sharing my perils with him, he felt the best remedy was to hit the airport bar. Drinks led to dinner and eventually to my hotel room. It was the most

memorable three day rendezvous. I don't know how I even got any work done."

While patrolling the airport, don't forget the bars. Women nursing cocktails in the lounge are usually a good indication of a flight delay. Better still, the dreaded cancellation due to bad weather. Most travelers who have been grounded indefinitely are usually distraught. Once again, it's time for Sir Lancelot to ride to the rescue.

Christine, 38, Advertising Executive, Los Angeles, California

"On a recent business trip to Chicago, my return flight was cancelled due to a snow storm. While having a drink, I got into a conversation with a young man seated next to me. Within the hour, we left the bar and checked into an airport hotel. We had an incredible time together. If I didn't have to go back to L.A., I surely would have delayed my flight for another day!"

Danielle, 36, Pharmaceutical Sales, Dallas, Texas

"The same thing happened to me in Denver. This guy was something else. He was a wonderful lover and fulfilled my fantasies. I can't wait until next month when I have to go back to Denver."

Patrolling the airport can definitely have its advantages. If nothing else, now you know why they call it a layover.

Hotel Bar- I find that tourists can be one of the more lucrative groups when it comes to scoring. This is because they are on vacation and looking for some fun and excitement. Besides, they are in a strange place, where no one knows them.

Hotel bars are also a great place to meet business travelers. Traveling by yourself can be lonely. Approach her right and she'll

85

welcome the company.

What if she just closed a big deal and there's no one to celebrate with? That's when you step in.

Molly, 29, Advertising Executive, Los Angeles

"I was on business in New York City. Would you believe that in a city of eight million people, I was lonely. I just didn't want to be alone. While sitting in a hotel bar, I met this cute guy. He not only showed me Central Park, he showed me a few other things as well."

Wanda, 23, Public Relations Executive, Chicago, Illinois

"I just had lunch with clients at the Drake Hotel. After closing my first big deal, I really wanted to celebrate. After what I thought would be a quick drink in the hotel bar, I began chatting with a guy. A couple of drinks later, we were feeling no pain. What a weekend! I wonder who'll be the lucky guy when I close my next big deal!"

Hotel bars can be a great place to meet women, however, beware of hookers. They often cruise hotel bars, doing what you're doing. Only they expect to get paid.

In this chapter we've explored some obvious, as well as not so obvious, places to meet women. From the women that I've interviewed, we've learned that these places are ideal for scoring.

Always be on the alert. The girl of your dreams may just be around the bend. If not, perhaps she will at least be "miss right now."

Chapter Ten

How To Sleep With Your Workmates

"Noblesse oblige. Rank has its responsibility."
A very wise man

"Work is the cure of the drinking classes."
Oscar Wilde

You spend countless hours at the office hoping to climb the corporate ladder. All work and no play? Do you fear becoming a dull boy? Has sexual frustration gotten the better of you?

Think twice before you consider the women at the office. I don't care how attractive or willing they are, you could be headed for a downfall. If nothing else, heed the advise of that very wise father to his son, "Don't ever shit where you eat."

My rule for office romances is quite simple. DON'T DO IT!! The fucking you get, may be your own. Once you start an affair, it can only end in one of two ways. You will either break up or get married. Considering the choices, I don't care for either nor the consequences.

Don't forget that you also run the risk of getting fired. Not to mention the possibility of being charged with sexual harassment.

According to a recent survey by Stuff Magazine, fifty-one percent have confessed to an affair with a co-worker. What I find even more amusing is the same survey found that thirty-five percent of those liaisons were with the boss.

Dating a co-worker could definitely be hazardous to your wealth. However, no one seems concerned with job security. Let's take a look not only at scoring in the office, but how to get away with it.

Leah, 26, Payroll Clerk, Anaheim, California

"I used to flirt shamelessly with a guy from customer relations. We were always discreet and one night we decided to take the plunge. For the last three months no one is the wiser of our secret affair."

A word of caution. Be careful when you flirt at work. If she isn't receptive to your advances it could be dicey.

Jane, 24, Copier Sales, Cincinnati, Ohio

"At the risk of sounding conceited, if he's cute, it's flirting. If he's unattractive, it's harassment. I've had a couple of trysts with guys from work. Of course we kept it very discreet. After all, I'm not the office slut."

My best advise on flirting with a co-worker is of course, to be discreet. The safer you play it, the better off you'll be. Never put anything in writing. That's right, no love notes or e-mails.

Shari, 30, Public Relations, Palo Alto, California

"Once I had a fling with one of my co-workers. He sent me an e-mail detailing how much he enjoyed it when I gave him head. Big mistake! He accidentally sent it to the general company list."

It's imperative that you understand her biggest fear. Gossiping co-workers. No one wants to be the topic of discussion around the water cooler.

If you want to score, take it slow. Flirt discreetly and follow her lead. It is also advantageous to work late when she does. Working many hours together oftentimes fosters intimacy. I remember once during a staff meeting, how amusing I found the situation to be. If they only knew I had our boss on the conference table the night before. I could tell by the devilish eye she gave me that she couldn't wait 'till we were alone again. Imagine that, I was not only making the boss, I was also making over time pay. Time and a half as I recall.

Ruby, 36, Doctor, Boston, Massachusetts

"I do so love male nurses. They just rise and meet the challenge."

Cheryl, 42, Judge, Philadelphia, Pennsylvania

"I'm sure that male nurses are no more fun than law clerks. After all, my clerks are subject to my beckon call."

Now that you've decided to take the plunge, remember that office sex can get ugly. Referring back to the survey conducted by Stuff Magazine; fifty-one percent said that the best way to deal with a co-worker after having sex, is with more sex.

The safest co-worker to date is the temp. According to Dr. Judy Kuriansky, author of "The Complete Idiots Guide To Dating;" "They are in and out of the office with no messy strings attached."

Dr. Kuriansky also believes that it's best to take it slow. Find out when she's leaving, and try to date her on the way out. In this way you are sure to avoid any inter-office problems.

There are a couple of drawbacks when dating a temp. If she did a good job, she will most likely be calling back the next time a temp is needed. Worse still, she may even be offered a permanent position.

Lastly, my advice is to stay away from interns. Youth, beauty, inexperience, and naivete may be irresistible, but they only spell trouble. Who could ever forget the Washington, D.C. intern with a penchant for older men?

Chapter Eleven

The Bar Scene

*"Everyone starts out as strangers. It's where
you end up that counts."*
Rudolph Valentino

*"The more complex the mind, the greater
the need for the simplicity of play."*
Marquis de Sade

Before you skip this chapter and jump to the next, you could be passing on a lucrative area for womanizing. I realize that the bar scene is where most gents go and strike out, but don't give up yet.

Clubs are among the easiest places to score. If you've got game, you'll surely get the ladies.

Take my friend, Teddy Baxter. Teddy is the all-time champ at dance clubs. Why? He can dance! Although Teddy is only of average looks, glasses and balding, the women love him. The dance floor is his turf and that boy can move. Teddy is a professional dancer by trade and his dance card is always full.

Think back to the swashbuckler films of the thirties and forties. Tyrone Power, to be specific. Ty always played characters with an amusing personality, they were gallant, and as Zorro, he could dance. Antonio Banderas' rendition of Zorro could also dance. In fact, he danced his way right into Catherine Zeta-Jones' heart.

Kim, 25, Photographer, San Francisco, California

"I love to dance. It's a pity that most men can't dance or just flat out refuse to. The guy who can strut his stuff on the dance floor can dance his way to my bed anytime."

Katrina, 29, Customer Services, Huston, Texas

"If he can move on the dance floor, he can move in bed. Need I say I more?"

If dancing just isn't part of your repertoire, don't give up on the clubs. You can always take lessons. That's how I learned how to Swing dance. I also met a lot of women while taking classes.

Happy hours are perhaps my favorite haunts. Think about it.... Women abound, food is free, and drinks are half price. Now what could be better?

Terri, 30, Sales Rep. Seattle, Washington

"I like meeting men at happy hours. Everyone is pretty kick-back after a hard day's work. It's also a much easier environment to carry on a conversation."

Janice, 27, Paralegal, St. Louis, Missouri

"I especially like happy hours. It's nice to have a drink after work and unwind. If I meet a guy in the process, so much better. I also feel safe at a happy hour. It's still early and I don't feel like I have to go with a bunch of girls."

Joann, 31, Insurance Adjustor, St. Paul, Minnesota

"I love TGIF! I'm with friends and co-workers and we party! Sometimes I even find myself waking up in a strange bed. Oops, I can't believe I admitted that."

I guess because I'm single, I frequent happy hours and clubs. I date a lot of waitresses and bartenders. My friends are amused by how I tip. Twenty percent, I'm pursuing her. Thirty percent, I'm dating her. Fifty percent.... I've scored.

Isn't that expensive you ask? Not really. I get a lot of free food and drinks. And with their hectic schedules, we usually go out no more than once a week.

How To Pick Up A Hot Bartender

The most important thing to remember when going after that gorgeous bartender is timing. You must first and foremost understand, that unlike you, she's working. It is imperative for you to approach her when the bar is fairly empty. If you don't heed this warning, the only thing that you'll be looking forward to is the drink your angel just served you.

It's much better to come early. The bar will be slower and she'll have more time to talk. Also target slower nights, like Tuesdays and Wednesdays. I have also found that it's better to strike up a conversation when no one is waiting for a drink. Since she may have to cut you short to wait on them.

Keeping all of these obstructions in mind, it's best to be quick-witted and upbeat. Make pithy observations about your surroundings, or tell her amusing, but brief anecdotes. As for myself, poetry works the best. I know it might sound ridiculous, but remember, women love to be romanced.

Seduce Me!

Shannon, 29, Bartender, Ventura, California

"We sure do love being romanced. I work at an upscale restaurant on the beach and one night this good-looking guy sat at the bar and ordered a drink. It was a slow night and we got to chatting. From his opening words, he compared me to the heroine in a poem. Coincidentally, I was familiar with the verse. As the evening rolled pleasantly along, he held me spellbound. He always knew the right things to say and when it should be said. By night's end, I was ready to give out my phone number, but he didn't ask. He just wanted to know when I worked again. Once that was settled, he assured me that he would drop in for a drink. I was as giddy as a schoolgirl anticipating his return. Shortly thereafter we became lovers. It lasted for about a year and then his company transferred him to Chicago."

Remember, don't get pushy. Though you may believe your bartender is Heaven sent, to her you are just another thirsty customer.

First and foremost, you have to stand out. Does buying an endless supply of drinks work? Absolutely not! You will convince her that you are nothing than a pathetic drunk.

You're sure to impress her much more buying rounds for your friends and other customers. It leaves her with the impression that you are the good guy. Especially if you also buy a drink for her. Don't forget other employees of your new found watering hole. Not only will they be impressed, you now have some allies who are sure to come to your aid.

Nevertheless, everyone will keep drinking which translates into more tips for her.

When ordering drinks, don't ask for her advice and don't ask for some complex libations. Ordering a Lemon Drop or a Hawaiian Rainbow tells her that you are nothing more than a high-maintenance wuss.

Yvonne, 32, Bartender, Portland, Oregon

"Exactly! This guy used to come in and always try to stump me by ordering some complex drinks. I guess he thought he was cute and it was his way of flirting. It took a while, but once he realized that I wasn't having fun, he didn't return. I pity the bartender he's now harassing. I'll bet she's had to mix some crazy concoctions like a Cosmos Spritzer or a Brain."

If ordering colorful drinks isn't the way to your angel's heart, is buying a myriad of straight whiskeys the answer?

Once again...no. Being a lush is not the way to her heart. The best way to seduce her is simply to put her at ease. Become friendly and make your move from there.

Heather, 27, Bartender, Palm Springs, California

"I couldn't agree more. I work at a popular golf resort. The fellow that always catches my eye is the one with a personality. You know the type. He's a gentleman who has great rapport with his friends and others. He's the one who enjoys celebrating with a few drinks after 18 holes."

What about the double entendre drink? Will she find this witty, urbane and bold? Get a grip! Asking her for a "Screaming Orgasm" or a "Slow Comfortable Screw" will only put you in the category of JERK!!

Molly, 34, Bartender, Hollywood, California

"All I can say is immature creep! You'd better watch it because it's not my ass you'll be caressing, but my spike heel upside your head."

Seduce Me!

Dawn, 30, Bartender, Seattle, Washington

"I can't believe how immature most guys are. They just have no idea on how to approach a woman. I'll bet the only action these dogs are getting is from their own two paws."

Sara, 35, Bartender, Santa Barbara, California

"I know exactly the type. The bar I manage is frequented by all of the college kids. They fancy themselves "too cool" when they whisper throatily to me that they'd like a Slow Comfortable Screw."

Terri, 28, Bartender, Tucson, Arizona

"I'll go you one better. I hate when the chumps ask, 'How much for a Slow Comfortable Screw?' "

Renata, 26, Bartender, Channel Islands Harbor, California

"Tourists can be just as bad. They think that just because they are in town for a couple of days, we're pulling up our skirts just to go sailing on their boats."

All things considered, how then should we tip our mixologists of ambrosian elixirs? Tip well, but consider it a long-term investment. Tipping big means she'll remember you. It doesn't mean that she'll take you home. SPECIAL BULLETIN!!! She's a bartender, not a prostitute.

I'd also like to caution you with regard to over aggressiveness. Get too forward and the only person interested in your advances will be the behemoth posted at the front door.

So play it cool. Be polite and display confidence. Heed these words and you are sure to impress your one and only love.

Tawny, 27, Bartender, Phoenix, Arizona

"Oh yeah...learn how to approach and impress me, and I'll take you home for a "Slow Comfortable Screw" every time."

Gents... need I say more?

Seduce Me!

Chapter Twelve

Friends With Benefits

"Never make an enemy when you can just as easily make a friend."

Julius Caesar

"Too much of a good thing can be wonderful."

Mae West

In many ways this chapter could be the most important. A friend with benefits is the perfect relationship for most men. Consider the advantages. A woman whom you like to hang out with. She also likes to go to sporting events. Better still, she keeps up with the guys at the happy hour. WHAT A WOMAN!

How then do we talk one of our female friends into becoming a friend with benefits? How do we impress upon her that such a relationship is mutually advantageous?

Begin with the obvious, you must both be unattached. Foremost, you must always be honest with her. You absolutely cannot mislead her in any way just to get laid. Women place a great deal of value on their male friends, so don't blow it.

Her initial fear will be for your friendship. Will fooling around jeopardize the bond you have between the both of you?

Assure her that you are friends first and will always remain such. After all, you value her friendship above all else. Your sexual relationship is a convenience for the both of you. Remember, women need a reason to have sex, men just need a place.

If she's dating, she'll end up in bed with someone she had no intention of ever sleeping with. How did this happen? Gents, special bulletin... women get horny too!!!

The dilemma for women is when to have sex with a man. Most women feel that if she puts out to soon, the guy will think that she's a slut, and won't call her back. Worse yet, he'll call only when he's horny. Most guys assume that once they get it, they can call whenever they are in the mood.

Keeping these factors in mind, a relationship with you begins to show merit. However, it's important to establish the ground rules. What, besides sex do each of you hope will come from your relationship?

Most men would be in favor of minimal entanglement. Men prefer to do without the cuddling or sleeping over. For men, intimacy is having sex. Rest assured that your friend with benefits will quickly tire of this liaison.

Two things must be considered for the relationship to succeed, how will you make her feel special? And will you do things without her getting attached?

Remember, for women, once they start having sex regularly with one person, they are prone to emotional attachment. It's difficult for most women to give themselves without feeling anything.

It's imperative that you retain strong friendship ties. She needs to know that just because you've begun sleeping together, she won't run the risk of losing a valued friend.

I've found that by doing the little things that matter to her, as any friend should, will make all the difference in the world. I would also recommend that you keep the relationship to yourselves. Don't cheapen the relationship with beer hall gossip with your male buddies.

Darcy, 28, Copywriter, Los Angeles, California

"I had a relationship with my best friend. It was great! We were always there for each other. Eventually, we both pursued other love interests. But I'll always treasure our secret time together."

Roxanne, 31, Secretary, Denver, Colorado

"My best friend and I carried on for a while. It was somewhat difficult when he got married. His wife was okay with our little tryst, which didn't surprise me. She's one of the finest people that I've ever known. In fact, she and I have also become the best of friends."

Diane, 34, Customer Care, Tempe, Arizona

"My guy and I carried on for quite some time. We eventually moved on, but I don't regret out time as lovers. Five years later, we're still the best of friends."

What if she wants to keep your dalliance to one night? Fine. You're not hurt and you won't hurt her. Out of respect, don't push her for an encore performance. Should it happen again, *c'est la vie*. Take it for what's worth and carry on with the friendship as usual.

Seduce Me!

Monica, 25, Dental Assistant, Laguna Hills, California

"A couple years ago I had a bad break up. My best male friend was there for me. It was a night of passion that I will never forget. After that our relationship carried on as before, yet there are times when we both recall our night together with a risqué smile and a wink."

Callie, 30, Project Coordinator, McLean, Virginia

"Last year, everything that could go wrong in my life happened. My closest friend took me away for a weekend. After that I was ready to take on the challenges ahead of me. He's still my friend and he's still in my corner."

All of the examples that the women on our panel have given have been quite positive. This is because all of the male friends were considerate of the women's feelings and situations. I would once again stress that you do not lie or try to take advantage of your friend's woes. Exploiting her troubles in the quickest way to lose a valued friend.

Camille, 35, Journalist, Ventura, California

"I had a rendezvous with a guy whom I thought was my friend. No sooner than he was out of my bed, he's bragging to his buddies. To him, I was just another conquest."

Alana, 26, Actress, Burbank, California

"This bastard did the same thing to me. It seems that men will sacrifice a friend if they think they're going to get laid."

What if you both feel you made a connection? Is it feasible to pursue a relationship together?

Like anything else, it depends on the people involved. For

some individuals, falling in love with your best friend is the ideal match. For others, it can only spell catastrophe.

Wendy, 31, Retail Sales, Cleveland, Ohio

"I married my best friend and it's been absolute bliss. I love that he knows and understands me totally. So much for the notion that men and women can't be friends."

Sheila, 29, Designer, Miami, Florida

"I married my pal. I love his patience and understanding of my moods. I think that the only way he could have learned how to deal with me was by being my friend first."

Jill, 32, Office Manager, Philadelphia, Pennsylvania

"The exact opposite happened to me. It seems that friendship alone is not enough to build a life together. I guess we both wanted more passion. Since we could not find it at home, we both carried on with extra-marital relationships. Eventually we divorced and are no longer friends. How could we be?"

Dagmar, 28, Retail Management, Berkley, California

"My marriage ended the same way. We just took each other for granted until we drifted apart. Thank God we didn't have any children."

Divorce on any level is unfortunate. It can be catastrophic when you lose not only your spouse, but your best friend as well.

Speaking from my own personal experience, I married my best friend. Eventually we divorced. We're still on friendly terms, but our relationship will never be the same.

On a positive note, I currently have a friend with benefits. The dalliance has been marvelous. The difference is that we take the sexual part of our relationship for what it is and nothing more.

Epilogue

"You can't change beliefs, only believers."
Bismark

"If you meet with triumph and disaster and can deal with each of these imposters in the same way, you will be a man my son."
Rudyard Kipling

Well gents, there you have it. We have explored the topic of meeting and seducing women at length. If you want to have more "Ms. Right Nows" in your life, just go for her.

I don't mean to over simplify the issue because as we all know, nothing simple is ever easy. However, it is up to you, and you alone, to change your dating life.

You've got to clear all emotional blocks and change limiting beliefs. Release the "should have" and "yeah buts," from your life. Remember, whatever you are looking for is looking for you.

We judge ourselves by our intentions. Others judge us by our actions. I encourage you to initiate change in your life.

As always, I will close with this from Guillaume Appollinaire:

"Come to the edge," he said.
They said, "We are afraid."
"Come to the edge," he said.
They came.
He pushed them.
And they flew.

The End

Of

Seduce Me!
What Women Really Want

R. Gregory Alonzo will return with

Seduce Me!
Why Men And Women Cheet

About The Author

R. Gregory Alonzo is a best-selling author who has been featured on several radio and television talk shows across the country. He is listed in Who's Who in America and is constantly in demand for public appearances.

Greg is a sports car and wine enthusiast and collector of contemporary Asian art. He resides in Santa Barbara, California.

Readers interested in reaching Greg for a personal appearance or a product catalog may contact him at:

Chambers Books
556 S. Fair Oaks Ave. Ste. 313
Pasadena, Ca 91105
866-482-9739 (Toll Free)

Other titles by R. Gregory Alonzo
published by Chambers Books

- Say Yes To Success

Personal Notes